My Word Is My Bond

Cool cowboy sayings from the heart to get you through life

CODY HARRIS

Copyright © 2018 Cody Harris

All rights reserved.

DEDICATION

This is a heartfelt wish to the reader and why this book means so much to me.

The cowboy way of life has been so rewarding. I have been blessed enough to make a living doing something I love while living a lifestyle that is somewhat of a forgotten code. Being a cowboy has helped me find joy and peace. The joy comes from loving what I do and the peace comes from knowing I am making a positive impact on the present, and more importantly, the future.

If you could take away one thing from this book I pray it would be this: a cowboy isn't something you do, it is who you are! Whether you come from a big city or a small town like me, anyone can choose to live like a cowboy. The lessons and thoughts in the pages of this book can be applied to anyone in any walk of life. I hope you can take them to heart and remember, anyone can follow, it's up to a cowboy to lead!

Keep in mind that I am no writer and have a very short attention span. The length of this book reflects that! Writing is just not something they teach at the "School of Hard Knocks." I wanted to produce something that my son could one day read and say, "You know what? My dad was a cool character." I wanted to share something simple that would bring a grin to his face, so hopefully, he could do the same for someone else.

CONTENTS

	Acknowledgments	i
1	Cowboys Were the First Superheroes	Pg. #1
2	Cowboy Cool	Pg. #14
3	Cowboy Contract	Pg. #24
4	Pull Your Hat Down	Pg. #34
5	Cowboy Love	Pg. #44
6	Cowboy Slang	Pg. #58
7	Jesus is a Cowboy	Pg. #64
8	Cowboy Common Sense (Dollar Stretcher)	Pg. #73
9	At the End of the Day	Pg. #81

INTRODUCTION

You can learn from an old bull like me.
I cannot remember a time when I didn't want to be a cowboy. The first time I saw a true cowboy was on the land I live, work and own today. His name was Bubba Cox. I was 10 years old when we pulled up on the property and I saw the silhouette of a man on a horse in the pasture. I thought wow, he's the real deal.

I already knew what I was. I knew I was a cowboy. But seeing Mr. Bubba resonated with me and for the first time I knew I was exactly where I needed to be. I grew up around cowboys my whole life, but Mr. Bubba was a cowboy in every sense of the word and he did not have to tell you.

I learned to rope with Mr. Bubba on his ranch for ten years before going off to college. I had always wanted my own beautiful piece of land like Mr. Bubba's and years later after he passed away, his family sold me this little piece of heaven. This is our ranch on the cover of this book.

So, what makes cowboys so intriguing? Cowboys always seem to be the coolest cats in the room. As a kid, I used to love to sit at our local diner in Robertsdale, Alabama, and listen to all the cowboys tell their tales of cow catching, rodeoing, or just a simple story with a cowboy twist.

Cowboys can spin a tale, now. They can turn a story about going to the dentist into a nail biting, gut-wrenching adventure. Even with a sad story a cowboy will draw you in.

There is no denying a cowboy. Most people you see walking down the street? You don't know what they do or who they are. That's not true of a cowboy. It's not just the hat and boots either. It's the way they carry themselves. Cowboys have an inner peace that shines through.

As far as I know there has never been a little girl or boy that didn't want to be a cowboy when they grew up. Maybe they saw a cowboy in a movie or at a rodeo; or maybe out of their car window in the middle of a pasture.

So many songs and countless movies have been made about cowboys. Poems, books, boots, streets, food and more all named for cowboys. It is the epitome of American culture.

So, what is it about a cowboy that captivates the hearts and minds of people? Is it the way they dress? Talk? Smile? Is it just the swagger and idea of a cowboy? If I was a betting man, I would say it is all the above. **It takes a lot of faith and sweat to be a cowboy,** and I reckon people notice that, and they want to know more.

I wrote this book to share with you some cowboy philosophies that have served me well. I hope you laugh, learn a few cowboy facts you never thought about, and maybe find some inspiration for your life.

It could get a little ranchy,

Cody Harris

CHAPTER 1

Cowboys were the first Super Heroes

My heroes have always been cowboys. Before Batman, Superman or Wonder Woman there was the cowboy. Roy Rogers was one of the first true super heroes. Throughout modern history heroes have evolved. If you watch movies today, Spiderman's suit has changed. Batman's suit has adapted. All the super heroes have been modified to fit our new imaginative world.

Cowboys have not changed. Cowboys still wear boots, spurs, pants, long sleeve shirts, vests and hats. Nothing has changed. It is not going to change.

Cowboys never lose sight of where they came from. They know where they're going is over there. They know where they came from is right here in their heart. They can't lose sight of where they came from to get to where they're going. They know from time to time they must look back to go forward. **You can be as lost as last year's Easter egg,** but if you look to your truth you will find your way.

These days it is sad when kids and people only look up to movie stars and sports stars as heroes. Folks idealize their heroes, right? They look up to them and try to pattern their lives like their heroes. If these folks were to look at the cowboy as their hero, (I don't mean the Hollywood version of the drunk, cussing, adulterous cowboy, but the true cowboy) we would be in a better place.

When I was a kid growing up I wanted to

be a garbage man. That was the coolest thing in the world to me. To be able to ride on the side of a truck going down the highway. I still feel that way about our everyday heroes. What if the trash man didn't come? I have dirty diapers right now. That guy is my hero when he pulls in my drive.

A true super hero is a single mother working two jobs to make ends meet. A hero is your everyday person working eight to five; a banker, lawyer, custodian, teacher, fire fighter or factory worker. Obviously, our soldiers are heroes. As a cowboy, those are my heroes. Without them, I couldn't do what I love to do for a living.

Why is the cowboy a hero to the world? I believe it is because he does not see himself as a hero. Cowboys just do what they do. The modern-day pop culture heroes put themselves on a pedestal. A cowboy looks at himself as being honored to be able to do what he does, and to serve his everyday superheroes.

The everyday working man or woman many times must sacrifice for their children or family. The cowboy does the same because he lives a selfless life. In modern day cowboy life our living is based off of markets that are controlled by who the heck knows what. It goes up. It goes down.

Some years you make money. Some years you lose. Most of the time you just try to break even. **Hills ain't nothing to a high stepper.** Cowboys don't do it for money. We do these selfless acts because if we don't take care of the land and we don't take care of the cattle who will?

If we don't promote the industry and uphold the traditional values of this industry and this lifestyle it is based on, no one else will. To me that is the essence of a true hero.

I know farmers that live this way. I talk to

many of them that go out and plant a crop knowing, *knowing* that they are going to lose money. They know for a fact that before they plant it they are going to lose money. The selfless aspect of this way of life is impressive of the human spirit to me. Those are my heroes.

Do you know why they do this? Why they plant essentially a profitless crop? Because, if they don't plant those peanuts or that corn who is going to do it? **Farmers feed America.** Without ranchers and farmers, we couldn't eat. Of course, if it weren't for the other everyday working heroes we wouldn't have anyone to feed. Cowboys wouldn't be stewards of the land if it weren't for other people to consume our labors.

If you have a pet, even one little fish, it takes a little bit of selflessness to feed that fish for it to survive. If another farmer, or rancher, or I decide one morning that I just don't feel like feeding 500 momma cows can you imagine what would happen? They wouldn't eat. I have to feed them.

If a farmer doesn't take the time to fertilize the grass, plant winter pasture or put out hay it doesn't get done. Cowboys are natural care takers and they do it humbly and generously. Is that not heroic? That is the hero quality that sets them apart.

In the Bible there is the parable of the lost sheep. The story goes that there are 100 sheep out there and one goes missing. The shepherd leaves his flock to find the one. That is a good definition of a cowboy. He will sacrifice everything for one. That is a hero.

All other super heroes we worship in our imagination or otherwise have super powers. A cowboy does not. Period. He is just a regular guy doing what he can. Cowboys fall from their horses. **They dust themselves off and get back on.** They don't have X-Ray vision or the power to fly. Superman had a cape and a cowboy has his hat.

Everyone falls off their horses at some point in their life. That can be a literal horse or a figurative horse. The thing about a cowboy is he always gets back on. I don't know how many people have literally been thrown from a horse, but it doesn't feel good. You lie there, with possibly a broken bone and seeing stars, and you have a choice. You can lie there and hope everything will be okay or you can get back on knowing that it might happen again.

The way I look at it is I can be thrown flat on my back, but at least I'm looking up and I can get up. That is the extra ounce of grit that makes a hero to me. I'm not talking about a gallon of grit. I'm talking about an ounce and that ounce is what makes the difference.

The saying goes, "Don't look a gift horse in the mouth." Cowboys don't. They don't underestimate their gift. They aren't looking them in the mouth either. They straddle their gifts back and ride. They ride whether it is good weather, bad weather, high tide, low tide, sun up, sun down, hell fire and brimstone all around. **It makes no never mind. They keep on going.** As Rocky Balboa said, "It's not how hard you hit. It's about how hard you get hit and keep moving forward."

I had a farmer call me one time to come rope a cow that was having complications giving birth. The cow had been in labor for a while and she was not happy at all. She was a Brangus cow and **high headed as a buck deer.** The farmer couldn't get her penned to pull the calf, so he called me.

I roped the cow. We threw her down and pulled the calf. Unfortunately, the calf was still born, but we saved the cow. Afterwards, the farmer said to me, "Wow, heroes really do come in all shapes and sizes."

I asked him what he meant, and he said, "I would have never got that cow held down by myself and ended up losing the cow and the calf. Here you are weighing a buck-20 soaking wet riding a 1,000-pound horse and caught her like it was a walk in the park."

I was about 17 at the time. I have since put on a few pounds but only in the places that count! I am now 160 pounds of **twisted steel and appeal.** Seriously, I had done something for that farmer that he couldn't do for himself. He saw me as a hero. I was the cow's hero as well. Although, she had a funny way of showing her appreciation. She politely tried to hook me when we got done pulling her calf. Ha!

Cowboys do this every day. I am not bragging on myself. I am sure there are cowboys out there that could have done it better and more efficiently. The point is, aren't these the types of acts we should see as heroic? Shouldn't cowboys be our superheroes? The save the day kind of fella or gal? You know, super heroes always have a disguise, so people don't know who they are. They don't hold a press conference and sign autographs after every act of kindness. So, why do they do it? Because that's what heroes do.

Heroes are prevalent in the sport of rodeo. Bare back and saddle bronc riding are old traditional ranch style events where cowboys get on bucking horses and judges score the event. When the horses quit bucking and the eight second whistle goes off the cowboy has three options: he can either get off, fall off or rely on the "pick-up" man.

The pick-up man is the hero. He is the knight in shining armor that can sweep in to help. That bareback or saddle bronc rider is going to hit the ground going 35 miles an hour from a 16 hands high horse. That's a pretty good fall. **It**

could make a bunny rabbit slap a bobcat.

The pick-up man runs along the bucking horse and the bareback or saddle bronc rider jumps off the bucking horse onto the pick-up man's horse and holds on for dear life. The pick-up man gets that rider to a safe part of the arena and sets him down. That is the epitome of a hero.

Imagine being on a thousand-pound animal running across an arena with only one intention in that animal's DNA, to buck you off. All good bareback or saddle bronc riders love a good pick-up man. He saves them trips to the hospital, broken bones and more. He is a hero to all rodeo cowboys.

Another hero of the rodeo is the bull fighter. Bull riders who entertain people all over the world in arenas and on TV wouldn't ride bulls if it weren't for the bull fighters. These are the guys that when the bull rider gets bucked off or the ride is over avert the bull's attention from hooking the rider.

Everybody calls them a rodeo clown. He is not a clown. He's a bull fighter. The clown is the guy that keeps everybody amused during slack time with a performance. The modern-day bull fighter's job is to get hooked by a bull or get run over by a bull, so the bull rider doesn't. His job is to step in front of a freight train for his brother, friend or cousin. He can get broken, he's making less than the person riding the bull and he's the one taking the lick! He is an unknown hero. I compare the bull fighter to Clark Kent. He didn't want the credit for saving the day but when he was called, he went.

You see that heroes can come in all shapes and sizes, from different backgrounds and different walks of life. But if you will dig down deep inside I'd be willing to bet your first hero was a cowboy!

A hero can be anyone you look up to that adds

value to the human condition through acts of sacrifice and kindness. Cowboys are an example of this and if you look in your heart and memory will discover they were your first super heroes.

CHAPTER TWO

Cowboy Cool

Cowboys are cooler than a cucumber. I think everyone knows that. Why? I believe the number one reason is the way they handle situations and carry themselves. Cowboys don't cry over spilled milk. They don't sweat the small stuff. **They keep their head on a swivel, stay cool and try not to get kicked in the teeth.**

Let's take politics as an example. Cowboys know that politicians bicker and carry on. The policies they dictate don't control the true outcome. Cowboys don't spend their time worrying about tomorrow because, as the Bible says, tomorrow will worry about itself. They know that at the end of the day all the hustle and bustle and worry in this world is a trap that can only get to you if you let it.

There is an identity crisis in America. People don't know who they are, or they are unhappy with who they have become. It is pretty simple for a cowboy. **Once a cowboy always a cowboy.** Cowboys are doing what they love on this earth and when we die we know we will be doing what we love in heaven. We know that we are going to inherit the largest ranch there is.

When you watch a cowboy movie and a gun fight ensues you can always tell who is going to win by who is the calmest and the coolest. Most of the time in competition or life in general, your biggest enemy is yourself. I am as guilty as the next person of getting all nerved up about a situation and not seeing the forest for the trees. It doesn't take but a second to make a mountain out of a molehill.

One day, on the way to a rodeo, about three hours out, we had a blow out on the truck. We couldn't find a tire store. When we finally found a tire, we couldn't find a jack. When we found a jack, we couldn't find a tire tool. Basically, **we couldn't find our butts with both hands and we looked like a couple of monkeys riding a basketball.** When we finally got the tire changed and back on the road we still had a three-hour drive. The Rodeo started in two hours.

I am in the back seat about to give myself a heart attack from worry. My cousin Quin was **running double nickels in the hammer lane** on the interstate. I was fit to be tied. I couldn't hold my tongue any longer. I said, "Quin, **the gas pedal is on the right**. Why don't you bear down a little bit harder? We got to get."

Quin just rolled his eyes. "Cody, no matter where you are going, there you are." Cowboy cool. It was a few more years before I understood what my cousin said to me. It doesn't matter. Do the best you can. It won't happen until you get there.

Believe it or not, they were dragging the arena a few minutes before the rodeo started. The tractor ran out of fuel. It took them 45 minutes to move the tractor out of the arena. **Well, I'll be dipped in glue and rolled in bread crumbs.** We made it on time. Lesson: it all works out in the end. I had spent the last 180 miles with a stomach full of my chewed nails. Meanwhile, my cousin Quin, was cowboy cool.

I was attending a rodeo in Alexander City, Alabama, one day. It was a few hours before the rodeo started. My uncle was putting it on and I was up there helping him, picking up bucking horses, trying out bulls and competing.

I was probably 16 at the time. I thought I was a hot commodity. **I thought I was sexier than socks on a rooster.** I had a new truck. I was winning. We were sitting around, and this pretty girl came walking by. She had one of the prettiest cow dogs I had ever seen. It was an Australian Shepard.

She was leading this dog with a leash. I remember thinking, what am I going to say to this girl? How am I going to get her attention? I wanted to flirt with her. I wanted to get the conversation going. All I could think of was, "Ma'am, that sure is a pretty dog."

My Uncle Bo was sitting right there beside me. He just kind of looked up slowly and said, "What dog?" It took me a minute to realize what he had done. He totally won that one. I was definitely his wingman and not the winner.

I had never seen anything so cool. He didn't even hesitate. This is the essence of cowboy cool. To this day that might be the coolest thing I have ever witnessed. I would have been the third wheel on that date for sure!

Cowboys are witty. But more than that they aren't in a hurry, especially to deliver a line. They take life as it happens and live in the moment. There is nothing but the moment, the now. **Don't start a car and you can't drive no where.** This applies to fighting but also to meeting a pretty girl. If you don't strike up the conversation you will never get that first date. I learned a lot from my uncle that day.

You know, a cowboy may talk slow but that doesn't mean he thinks slow. I think these days people get so caught up in the rush. Go, go, go. **But, cowboys know that slow is smooth and smooth is fast.** The earth turns at the same speed for all of us. Booger always says, "**People get so caught up in this life they can't tell the difference in pig poop and wild honey.**" So true. I've seen it with my own eyes.

This one time I was in Montana. It was breathtakingly cold. **I'm as country as cornbread** now, and I have never been in this kind of cold in my life. There was a barn that about 50 people were standing behind. We were huddled up, taking shelter from the wind. I'm from south Alabama. I was not dressed for this weather. I was in my jeans and pearl snapped long sleeve shirt.

My teeth were chattering. This cowboy looked at me. He called me "Country." He said, "You cold, Country?" I said, "I sure am. I'm freezing." He said, "Well, it could be raining." That is a cowboy. Everyone encounters positive and negative in their life. It is not what happens to you but how you react to the situation you encounter.

At the end of the day if you are healthy, your family is healthy, you have a roof over your head and food in your belly, what more do you have to worry about? Cowboys strive for this contentment, this cowboy cool. I have met many a cowboy that didn't know where their next rodeo entry fee was coming from, but they were happy.

The world is changing. Cowboys go with the flow but remain true to their nature. I had this great idea that we should put GPS tags on our cattle. We spend so much time with our dogs searching for lost and run-away cows why not speed the process up with technology? Well, Booger had a different idea.

Booger made me realize that some things can't be changed. Some things work the way they work. End of story. **You can drive 10,000 miles in your car but it ain't going anywhere unless you put gas in it.** As it turns out, those cow dogs are **pretty durn handy.**

They used to drive cattle by horseback and

ship them by trains. Now cattle can be in a feed yard hundreds of miles away in a matter of hours deposited by a semi-truck. At the end of the day you still must have horses to gather the cattle. The modern world has worked its way into the cowboy world. But the basic grass roots of cowboy life have not changed, and they won't. Cowboys are somewhat of a conundrum. They are trying to hold onto and preserve a way of life, and yet trying to keep up with the present and the future.

In our current world we have fertilizers and GMOs and all types of modernization to keep up with the demand of our society. But the foundation of seed to soil to bear fruit has not changed, and **the key to building something good is a solid foundation.** This is true of farming and the coolness of cowboy life. Start strong, don't try to reinvent the wheel and keep it cool.

Cowboy cool is a way of life. It is the essence of knowing your truth, living in the moment, and looking on the bright side of any situation. When in doubt think, what would a cowboy do?

CHAPTER THREE

Cowboy Contract

I like that kind of pressure. In this day and time, it seems that a man's word doesn't mean what it used to. Back in the day when you gave someone your word it was as good as swearing on the Bible. An oath should not be broken. I take that very seriously.

I won't lie to you. I have broken my word before. But the older I get the more I realize your word is your bond, and you are only as good as that.

A few years ago, I drove to north Mississippi for a rodeo. I was meeting with a small committee of great people, the kind I grew up with. We walked around the arena meeting people, shaking hands and kissing babies. After I had seen what I needed to we went into a small office to get down to business.

I was a little nervous because this was a first-year rodeo with a brand-new committee and that can be good or bad. The good side is they were young and hungry and not scared to get out there and **shake the bushes** to get the sponsors and spectators we needed.

The bad side is that they were inexperienced and may have bit off more than they could chew. Sitting down, we discussed numbers and I told them my bid. They agreed to my terms. I reached for my briefcase to pull out a pre-fab contract and the main dude, a cowboy, says, "Son, we don't need that. How about **a**

cowboy contract?" He stuck out his hand to shake.

On the way home, I thought I should have had them sign a contract. This rodeo is seven hours from my house. It would be a disaster if they didn't pay. Then I remembered a cowboy's word is his bond. If they don't have that, they have nothing.

An old timer once said to me, "**If I tell you a rooster has a can of snuff. You better look under his wing.**" It is tough to take another person's word, especially when it comes to money. We all know, as the saying goes, that money is the root of all evil. But as a cowboy that example would be unsettling if we couldn't give and take another man's word for what it is. There is only one place a rooster can hide snuff. He doesn't lay an egg like a hen. So, if a cowboy tells you something you better believe him.

In the cattle business, "A man is his

word," is the most important cowboy code we can live by. For example, let's say I call someone in the panhandle of Texas and tell them I have a load of heifers to sell. I tell him they are going to weigh 750. They're going to be 75% black, 15% Charolais, and 5% sprinkled reds. At the end of the day that guy has no idea if what I just told him holds any clout.

He doesn't know if I told the truth or not. He has not seen the cows. Unless you have a past relationship with a customer they can only take your word for it. This new customer doesn't know me from Adam, and I'm going to load about $70,000 - $100,000 worth of cattle on a semi and drive 15 hours to Texas. His word better be good.

The first time these cattle step off the truck is the first time this guy will ever see them. I am also taking his word that he is going to pay me for them. He's promising to mail me a very large check back to Alabama for the cattle. You can see why a cowboy contract is so important in this industry and in the cowboy world. The most significant thing in this business is your name and reputation. Your name is only as good as your word. Period.

An example of the greatest cowboy contract in our cultural history is when Captain Woodrow Call of *Lonesome Dove* gave his word to his best friend Gus that he would take his body thousands of miles from Montana back to Texas to bury him. People thought he was crazy, and maybe he was. But he had given his word, and that isn't taken lightly in cowboy culture.

Captain Call and his partner Gus were driving cattle from Lonesome Dove, Texas, to the Montana territory. On the way, his best friend, Gus, was killed. You can't just stop a 2,500-mile cattle drive to bury your friend. You can't stop the cattle.

Before Gus died he made Captain Call give his word that he would take him back to Texas to bury him. There was a little pecan orchard where he had met with his first love. It was a very special place to him near a creek bank.

In the movie, Captain Call says, "Why do I have to tote you all the way back there?" But Gus made him give his word that he would. So, when Gus died in Wyoming Captain Call had to preserve his body and leave him in Wyoming to finish the drive to Montana.

He wintered in the Montana town, getting the cattle settled and established. I am not sure how long he was there. It may have been a couple of years. But when all was set he headed back to Texas, stopping in Wyoming for Gus' body.

He toted him all the way back on his horse. 2,500 miles with a dead guy on horseback. When they arrive back in Texas and he gets Gus in the ground Captain Call states, "In the future I will be more careful about how easily I give my word." To me that is the epitome of a cowboy contract, and something I strive to live by.

I have lied, or rather, failed to abide by my word before. I am not perfect, and I am not proud to have gone back on my word. The most important action in that situation is to admit it and correct it. It is the only way to learn from your mistakes.

I gave my beloved Paw Paw my word and broke it once. He had been asking me to go fishing with him. I was spending so much time in the cattle and fencing business, working all the time, and my Paw Paw just wanted me to spend some time fishing with him.

I had given my grandfather my word that I would go with him to pull a log out of his favorite fishing hole. There was a big ol' piece of driftwood that had floated in to this hole. Paw Paw liked this particular fishing spot so much we named it after him.

"Paw Paw, I give you my word I am going to come help you." He would call me the next week. Same thing, "Paw Paw, I give you my word I'm going to come help you."

Well, before I could go get that fishing hole cleaned out my Paw Paw had congestive heart failure. He had COPD. He had to have open-heart surgery at 70 years old. He laid in the hospital for about three months.

I was out of town. My wife called me. I was in Los Angeles. She said, "I'm going to bump your flight up. You need to get back home. They are calling the family in. Paw Paw is dying." No one wanted to tell me. I was supposed to be on the west coast for a few more days.

I remember this devastating feeling in stomach. It wasn't that my Paw Paw was sick and possibly dying. It was that I had given him my word. I had promised him I would move that log and me and him would fish that hole. I broke it. It is times like that when **you have to keep your chin up, pull your hat down and be a cowboy.**

Thank God, my Paw Paw pulled through. He ain't no spring chicken but he is still getting around. I just remember that red eye flight home as terrible. The sickness in my stomach could not be described. I was praying the whole time and had faith that he would pull through. All of medicine said he was not going to make it. I honestly don't know if I ever could have forgiven myself if Paw Paw had died at that time.

I recruited a friend, and he and I went and cleaned that fishing hole out. It was a pretty, nice size job. Me and my Paw Paw, my other grandfather and my dad just took my son Carter there on his first fishing trip.

Right before Paw Paw had his open-heart surgery the last thing he did was give Carter a fishing pole. So, you can imagine that on the way home and the drive to the hospital were horrible. I was just in tears. Here I am, a cowboy, a man of God, and I broke my word to the man I love more than life itself.

Thank goodness things worked out. But, I tell you, I learned a lesson at that time. Do not give your word unless you mean it. Your word isn't a piece of candy, a business card or a free pen. Your word is something you need to stand by. If you can't honor it don't give it. It is and should be an oath. It is that simple.

Your word is your bond and an oath. When you give it to someone else stand by it. This will build your reputation as an honest person and soon you will be able to expect the same from others, as they will not want to let someone like you down.

CHAPTER FOUR

Pull Your Hat Down

Think long, think wrong. Have you ever thought about throwing it all in the trash and giving up? Most people have. Life can throw some curve balls your way. You can either throw your hat in the dirt, give up and walk away or you can **pull your hat down, pick your head up and be a cowboy.**

It ain't over till the fat lady sings. We all know nothing is over until it is really over. Billy the kid said it best, "There's many a slip between the cup and the lip." Billy and his gang were running from every type of law enforcement there was and about to be hanged when he said it. In modern times we say, "Don't count your chickens before their hatched. It ain't over till it's over."

This is a true cowboy thought process. I know it is obvious but on a daily basis most of us think the moment is reality. The truth is, **if you let the dust settle a little bit,** things may change. In all likelihood, things will improve.

At a calf roping one time I was talked into a friendly roping match. This is typically when two men or women see who the best roper is. Truth be told it is really who was best that day like most competitions. We didn't have a ton of money on the line: four head for $100 and the loser pays the stock charge.

I am so competitive I wouldn't have tried any harder if it was for a million bucks! We were tit for tat on the first two calves, but my third calf kicked, and I was running about fifteen seconds. That put me at about 7.1 seconds on my last calf to win the match.

Understand this, the fastest calf tied all day was 8.5 seconds. **I was more nervous than a long -tailed cat in a room full of rocking chairs.** I backed in the box, nodded my head and the next thing I remember was throwing my hands up at 7.1 seconds.

Some folks might call that luck and some folks might call that talent. I am leaning towards luck. But we all know that luck is when hard work meets opportunity. If that is true I will take luck over talent any day.

I have never liked the term "Cowboy up." I prefer, **"Pull your hat down and be a cowboy**." It essentially means "Just do it." Just like Nike says.

To literally do cowboy work you have to

pull your hat down so it sticks on to your head or it will fall off. The term is literal. But it is also figurative in our world.

Let's say you are out in a pasture. **It's raining like a cow peeing on a flat rock** and It is slick from raining all night. There's a bull out there that has to be caught. Who are you going to call? The professionals. You are the professionals. Mommy and daddy can't help you out of this one.

The only thing you can do in that situation is pull your hat down and be a cowboy. It is plain and simple. There is no time in a cowboy's working world for high fives. We can hug and kiss later. You just do the work when it is called for.

One of my favorite things in the Bible are the stories about many of the big figures like Job, or Simon, Peter, or Saul who became Paul who wrote quite a bit of the New Testament. Moses, a huge figure, is another one. These dudes had to work for it. Nobody was going to give it to them. **They had to suck it up butter cup and get it done.**

Rome wasn't built in a day either. Most of your successful people in modern life had to pull their hat down and be a cowboy. They just got to work. I love reading success stories, like Mark Cuban for example, who came from nothing and built an empire. Most of those huge successes have many stories of when life knocked them down, but they just pulled their hat down and got to work.

Life is not a sprint. It's a marathon. **We get so caught up half way through the fourth quarter throwing our sucker in the dirt and quitting**. If you take a cowboy approach to it, pull your hat down and get to work, who knows what will happen? Push through and watch the results.

I am going to share a pivotal moment in my life when I truly had to pull my hat down. I had gotten a rodeo scholarship to Oklahoma State College. My cousin Kyle, and my friend, Buddy Childress, all went to college together there.

Before we left our home town of Robertsdale, Alabama, our families all got together to eat at a local diner called Mack and Jerry's. It was a goodbye party. All the Moms and grandmas were crying. We were going to be attending school fifteen hours away.

The last thing my dad said to me before I left after, "I love you," was, "Don't get in a bind I can't get you out." I believe what he was saying to me was don't get out there and be stupid. Don't get broke or get hurt. You're on your own. It's time for you to pull your hat down and be your own man.

There I was at college not heeding what

my dad said. I got down and I got broke. I was in a major bind. I didn't have enough money to buy horse feed. Not cool.

What does that look like? I would go to a local restaurant at closing time that served fried fish. They would give me what I call "cracklings". The left over nasty, greasy junk floating in the fry oil. I would get a couple packs of ketchup and go back to our little apartment and pour that ketchup on the cracklings for supper.

I didn't want to call home and ask my parents for money. My parents had already sacrificed and done so much for me, I felt I was on my own and this was something I needed to figure out between me and God. I had to pull my hat down.

I decided to get me a fencing job. I wasn't winning nothing in rodeo. I was so broke and not winning that I had my head up my butt. **I needed a glass belly button.**

I think the glass belly button will be my next invention. You see, you take out your regular belly button and put this glass one in. That way when you are walking around with your head up your butt you can actually see where you're going.

I was at that point in my life. So, I got this fencing job. We were in this small town called Altus, Oklahoma, in the quartz mountains. Now I'm used to South Alabama dirt, sandy dirt, where you can dig a post hole real easy.

I bid the fence job to this guy in Oklahoma. I take a post hole digger out there and I am digging into rock on a mountain. I told this guy I would get the job done in a week. It took me a month. Humbled, to say the least.

That was when I said, "Alright. It's time to pull your hat down and get serious about what you're doing." Because, I don't want to be digging fence holes in the quartz mountains. But, **there ain't no quit in me.** So, I decided enough was enough and to dig myself out of this hole.

In hindsight, it was the best thing that ever happened to me because after I had to man up, so to speak, I went to winning. It took to being on rock bottom, bumming feed for my horses and rides to classes, and having to eat out of nasty restaurant paper sacks to pull my hat down.

I believe in life everyone needs to experience a rock bottom once to truly be able to rise to the top. You have to have your **egg cracked** to know what it's like to pull your hat down. I don't want anyone to intentionally get their egg cracked, but it does help to figure out what you need to do to get cracking.

There are several ways to crack your egg. There's truly cracking it, like getting bucked off a bull, and figuratively cracking it. Being thumped on the head by God and being humbled is one way to get your egg cracked. The bible says, the meek shall inherit the earth. Sometimes you need the rug pulled out from under you to comprehend your meekness and weaknesses.

At that time in my life I thought I was hot stuff. In college I thought I had the wind to my back and in my sails. Nothing could stop me. It took having my egg cracked to make me pull my hat down and be a cowboy.

Own your faults. Accept responsibility for yourself. If you pull your hat down and be a cowboy enough times, your life will eventually fall in to the place where it won't be necessary after every decision.

CHAPTER FIVE

Cowboy Love

It's time to saddle up and settle down. I don't know anyone with a heart so full of love as a cowboy. Whether it is love for a woman, love of freedom, love of the lifestyle, or love for our animals, cowboys give love.

Cowboy love is at its peak with God and family, but a very close third is our animals. The three animals that every cowboy has are horses, cattle and dogs. The love we have for animals is a respectful love. We respect the horses that carry us, the cattle that feed us, and the dogs that help us.

They all have a job to do and it's hard to have one without the other. The ranch equilibrium falls apart without all three. They all serve a very important purpose.

Whether you are in the rodeo business hauling stock across the country to produce a rodeo or a rancher with a cow/calf operation or feeder cattle, the well-being of the stock is your number one priority. That animal can not feed and water itself or give itself vaccinations or antibiotics when it's sick. It could be raining, snowing or **hotter than a two-dollar pistol,** the love the cowboy has in his heart for the livestock pushes him to set aside hardships and take care of what he has been entrusted with.

My sister and I used to get up before school and bottle feed calves. We didn't always want to as kids, but we were obligated to. If we didn't the calves wouldn't eat. It taught us responsibility and respect for the cattle we were taking care of and that were taking care of us. Of course, **respect is the other side of love.**

One of the things I love most is training a cow dog. I love getting that puppy and molding him or her in to the dog I need them to be. My wife and I raise Blue Heelers, and I'm here to tell you they are the most loyal and obedient dogs ever created.

I love to watch a puppy in training start to figure out what his job is. You don't have to train a Heeler puppy to push cattle. It's in their blood, in their genetic fabric, and they love to do it. You do have to train a Heeler puppy to come, to listen and to load up.

Just like being a cowboy isn't something you do, it's who you are. A Blue Heeler herding cattle isn't something the dog just does. It is who he is, and he does it well. They don't work cattle because we teach them to. They do it because they love it and it is what they were meant to do.

When I was 15 my dad took me and my cousin Kyle to a rodeo in Greensboro, Alabama. Ms. Linda Ray was there selling Blue Heeler puppies. Kyle and I bought one each. We left the rodeo that night and headed out to Tallapoosa, Georgia to another rodeo.

Along the way Kyle called his momma, Aunt Ruthy, to tell her he had bought a puppy. She was not very happy. So, when we got to Georgia Kyle found this pretty girl he had been smitten with for a while. He gave her the puppy.

You know what? He turned around and married that girl about 12 years later. They have a little boy named Trip and another one on the way. Now that folks, is a mixture of cowboy love and puppy love. **Any way you want to slice it, it don't get much better than that.** My cousin

Kyle has been to the National Finals Rodeo two times and I believe he is a future world champion steer wrestler.

I kept my puppy and named her Sister. As I am writing this she is sitting right here beside me, where she has been since I was 15 years old. I've never had an animal love me as much as she does. She's been to more rodeos and across more county and state lines than most people.

When I was in High School she would ride to school with me on the back of a truck. When we got there, she would jump down and sleep under the truck in the shade until I got out. **It could be hotter than two rabbits in a wool sock,** but she didn't care. She was right there with me.

"The secret to happiness is freedom. The secret to freedom is courage." – Thucydides

Cowboy love is about freedom. Freedom

in the form of working for yourself, not having to answer to anyone. Sometimes freedom is just an early morning sunrise on horseback looking over your cattle and land. That is a romantic scene I tell you. It takes courage to live the cowboy life. But courage leads us to the freedom we get to experience.

Sometimes freedom comes in the form of travel. The cowboy that rodeos for a living travels all over this great nation chasing a dream. Their sense of freedom comes from all the places they see and the people they meet.

One time I flew to Atlantic City, New Jersey, for a rodeo. I had a friend who knew a guy that knew a guy that had a horse up there I could ride. The night before I was at an amateur rodeo in Greenville, Alabama and the next day I was in Atlantic City. Now, you want to talk about a culture shock!

I am here to tell you, once again, I was as

lost as last year's Easter egg the whole time I was there. From the first cab ride of my life from the airport to the arena I was grinning. I thought, "This is love." I get to do this because I am a cowboy.

When I got to the boardwalk where the rodeo was to be held it was after midnight and it was locked down **tighter than a tick's behind.** So, I went to where any cowboy would, the casino! There I saw a few friendly faces and avoided having to sleep on a park bench. Which was a huge blessing because I would have **stuck out like a sore thumb.** Can you imagine? The cowboy life can take you anywhere.

Cowboy love can be defined in so many ways. It is easy for the perception of the cowboy to get twisted. Cowboys are ramblers chasing fast horses and pretty women, or vice versa. Many times, that is true. But cowboys are full of love and when the right woman comes along they are all hers.

One of the things I love about my life is waking up early. My wife will tell you we get up early in our house, before the sun is even awake. As they say, **the early bird gets the worm.** I'm here to tell you, I am not out looking for worms, but **in our world if you don't get up early you'll be sweating till late.**

There are other jobs in the world where the discipline to get up early is required. I darn sure appreciate them for that. I believe the good Lord only gives us so many hours in a day. What better way to start it then with a sunrise?

To some people that may mean just a start to another day. But to a cowboy it's an opportunity. It's a totally new beginning to a whole new adventure doing something we love. Now we may be belly deep in a trench digging a water line that day or we may be witnessing the birth of a new born calf. You never know what the day will bring.

That is another type of freedom. Freedom from monotony and freedom to be open to adventure. The love that drives us to get up and get going and see what the day might entail is the same love that gets us through whatever the day might require.

I was pondering the other day, and the older I get the better I get at it. I got to thinking how much people pay for an adrenaline rush or to escape reality. For instance, skydiving. My hats off to those folks. It is hard enough to get me on the plane much less, jump out of one. If I was forced to listen to 90's pop music or jump I would gladly stay seated and sing along.

The more I got to thinking about people buying an adrenaline rush the more I realized how lucky cowboys are. We get paid to get an adrenaline rush. It doesn't matter how many cows you've roped, how many rivers you've crossed, or how many horses you've broke. You still get a rush. If chasing a high horned Brahman cow across the highway, through a subdivision, and roping her at a drive through **doesn't get your pants stiff you better check your starch!**

My heart is thumping a little faster right now just thinking about it. I guess to some people chasing a cow seems crazier than jumping out of an airplane, and they might be right. You don't have to buy adrenaline or a high in my world. Some folks are walking around **higher than a hippie on a moped** and that is no way to live. Man, I love being a cowboy.

When it comes to love I feel that there are different levels. For instance, I love Taco Tuesdays! I am here to tell you that the meal of tacos is the greatest meal there is. I could eat it breakfast lunch and supper, which is dinner unless you're from the south, then it is supper! But it's still not the same kind of love that I have for a newborn baby calf or watching the sunset or rise on land that I have worked so hard to pay for. And yet, it still can't compare for the love that I have for my wife.

In January 2013, I was at the PCA finals in Biloxi, Mississippi. Typical finals, I was there to win, and nothing short of that. That is when I met my better half. I will never forget that day as long as I live.

On Thursday mornings, the morning before the first performance of the finals, you can ride your horse in the arena and kind of get acquainted with the ground. As I remember, I was riding my horse around, Ricky Jack was his name, and talking to everybody. I knew everyone! I looked up and I saw a real pretty girl that I didn't know. She was wearing a PCA finals jacket.

Everyone that makes the finals gets a PCA jacket. It is kind of like the masters. I remember that I could barely see her because her jacket was so big, and her cowboy hat was pulled down so tight that all I could see was her eyes and her nose. I remember thinking to myself, it is 70° in the south in January and she is dressed like it's -20 in Canada.

    I rode up to a good friend of mine, Miss Stephanie, and I asked her, "Who is that girl right there?" She said with a smirk on her face, "I was wondering when you were going to notice her." It is hard to believe, especially as small as the rodeo world is, which is less than half of a percent of America, that here is a girl that made the finals and went to the same rodeos as me, and I didn't know her!

    Heck, I know everybody in this business! Lord knows I am not bashful, so I rode up to her with the best grin that I could conjure up, and when she finally looked at me the only thing that I could say was, "Who are you?" She merely looked back at me and said, "Who are you?" '

I have never been at a loss for words. Not since kindergarten can I remember a time that I wouldn't argue with a judge about how something was spelled. It is a known fact that I can talk, but when that pretty, little dark-haired girl from Mississippi asked me who I was, I was speechless.

There are still moments to this day, when I look at my wife, that even Webster himself did not have a word to describe how I feel about her. I have been praying my whole life for a woman that could be my best friend. Someone I could do life with, the ups and downs, and someone who could put up with me! It seems God had a plan and knew that it wasn't going to happen until I met Misty. I had always heard about love at first sight. Heck, I'm a cowboy and a hopeless romantic. But, I am here to tell you, when I laid eyes on that woman, I was a **piece of butter hitting hot cornbread**... I just melted!

Love is the reason we are on this earth. If you show love for your family, love for your neighbor and love for animals it will be returned to you tenfold. Cowboys have big hearts and spread love all around. Try it and you will see.

CHAPTER SIX

Cowboy Slang

A man needs two of everything except a wife and a God. You need two dogs, two horses and two trucks. One of them is going to break down. Cowboy sayings and slogans are endless. We cowboys have our own language and probably need our own dictionary. Webster is missing out by not capitalizing on it. If you get two cowboys fired up and shooting the bull you're liable to need an interpreter to understand.

When you take directions from a cowboy you better learn quick and I mean really quick the distinct species of trees and which way is north, south, east and west. You need to know different breeds of horse and cattle and the assorted colors of structures. I don't mean red, green and blue. I'm talking cowboy colors like, "Turn up there by that house the same color as baby calf poop." That would be yellowish, by the way. You might get, "Turn up there by that bay colored barn." That is a horse color, kind of a maroon. Are you catching my drift?

One Saturday I was heading to a special heifer sale, and as usual, I was lost as last year's Easter egg. I finally saw a guy in a cowboy hat patching fence on the side of the road. I stopped and asked him how to get to the sale. He said, "Keep heading north right here for about five miles. When you get up there to the end of the pines on the west side of the road, turn left by that seven-strand barbed wire fence. I haven't figured out yet why they didn't just put up net wire instead of seven strands of barbed wire. Don't make a lick of sense. Head down that road around a few curves. Cross a bridge and when you're coming up that hill there will be a sway back Appaloosa off to your right. I guarantee it. She'll be standing there facing east. I guess she is waiting for the good Lord to come back. Turn right there and the sale will be down there on your right. But, drive slow cause there's a pack of ankle biters that can't pass up running out in front of you. You can't miss it!" Word for word, that is a direct quote.

Can you imagine? If you didn't know cowboy slang those kinds of directions might have led you to one of the places you see on the news where they got folks chained up in the basement. Just saying.

When someone is talented at sports you call them an athlete. In the cowboy world you are referred to as "**handy**." This basically means that you can get it done no matter what it is. They don't teach handy in schools because it can't be taught. You get to be a "hand" from experience. You get put in certain situations and just have to figure it out.

A cowboy could write an essay and draw a diagram on the proper way to load a cow in a trailer with your horse and a rope. The smartest nuclear physicist in the world could study it for years and years and still couldn't do it. There is no blue print to being handy. There isn't a permit you could pull or a work out routine you could do. **You just have to be baptized by fire.** You have to be thrown head first into the pool, not knowing how to swim, and make up your mind that you are not going to drown.

In many cultures and religions there is always a phrase that signifies that you agree with someone. In what little time I spent in the beautiful country of Canada I learned that they say, "Eh." I never really figured out in what manner they were using it. I just know I heard it everywhere. It seemed to stand for everything.

I go to church. When the preacher says something everyone likes we all say, "Amen." In that moment, "Amen," signifies that we agree with what the pastor is saying. If we didn't we would sit there on our hands and not say anything at all.

In the cowboy world you say, "**You bet!**" "You bet." Can be used so many ways it's kind of like a rope. You can rope an animal, drag stuff, heck, there are numerous ways to use a rope. The phrase "You bet," is just like that.

For instance, if a guy says, "You going to the rodeo this weekend?" I would answer, "You bet," unless he was older than me and then I would gladly say, "Yes sir. You bet." If somebody walks up and says, "Sure looks like it's going to rain." I would say, "**I'm no weather man** or you bet." Maybe I agree with him or maybe I don't know what else to say. "You bet," is always a nice fit.

"You bet," can also be a form or phrase like, "Amen." If someone does something **sure enough handy** you better believe **I will bare down on it** and say, "You bet!" So, you see this isn't an I bet, you bet situation, it's just you bet!

Language is an essential part of communication. Cowboys have a code or jargon all their own. How you communicate with others shows a lot about your integrity. God gave us two ears and one mouth. So, listen!

CHAPTER SEVEN

Jesus is a Cowboy

It's spring time year-round. Everything in our lives is growing and blossoming. Everything begins and ends with God. We have been taught that Jesus was raised by his earthly father, Joseph, to be a carpenter. I have strong proof that Jesus is a cowboy.

Before I go any further, please remember that I am a cowboy, and more importantly, a southern cowboy. So, I am going to tell this story just the way I would if I was there to see it.

The book of Mark: 11 is where I find this story. Jesus and his disciples were headed into town just returning from the country side proclaiming the gospel. Jesus tells two of his disciples to go on ahead in to town. He said, "There will be an unridden colt tied up. Bring that colt back to me. I am going to ride it in to town. "

Now think about that for a minute. Jesus is going to ride an unbroken colt with no saddle in to a crowd of hundreds cheering him on. From my personal experience trying to ride an unbroken colt, I would have been thrown before I climbed on. I believe most cowboys would agree you don't ride an unbroken colt into a crowd.

Most people would start with some round pen work, or maybe stick someone you don't like on the colt. Surely, there were some nice, broke donkeys, horses or camels in town. But that is not what Jesus asked for. He asked for the unridden colt, **and that's a whole new pair of boots.**

Maybe I am crazy, but I happen to think this is very significant. I believe Jesus was making a point. Not only is he the son of God but he is a cowboy.

This means so much to me personally. I have ridden bulls and horses in many a cheering crowd. When I read this about Jesus I truly identify with the son of God in myself. I am doing exactly what my father did. It gives me so much peace to know that my heavenly and earthly fathers are cowboys.

This is where it all started. This is where the foundation was set, and the torch was passed. Up to this point no one knew what a cowboy was because he didn't exist. On that Palm Sunday those folks watched a messiah ride in to town witnessing history's first cowboy.

I believe that if modern day folks could relate with Jesus on a personal level like I do it could help them lead the life they are supposed to by honoring him. It gives me a sense of peace to know who I am. A lot of people walk around this planet not knowing who they truly are.

We live in a world where everyone is out for themselves. If they would stop for a second to know their father, it would help them to know thyself. Knowing that Jesus is a cowboy helps cowboys to live like him. Not all of them follow him to a T, of course. Even his disciples denied him. But as a cowboy, it is cool to know that you are pretty much taking over your father's company.

Everyone is trying to gain purchase on this earth. Buying this house and that car and more. All you are really doing is leasing it. Because you can't take it with you when you go. It doesn't belong to you.

I walk around with a smirk on my face about this. It reminds me of show and tell in grade school when kids bring their parents to school to brag about them. Well, my dad is a cowboy.

People bicker these days about politics and everything under the sun. I just smile at that. It inspires me to know that I am doing exactly what my father did. In a world where people don't know their true identity, I know who I am because of who my father before was. **I don't need a mansion to be happy. I don't need the fastest car. If I have my truck, my dog and a good set of horses I am happy.**

I was comforted by Jesus as a cowboy before I could read the Bible. When I was a kid I had to endure several lung surgeries. I was about five or six years old. I remember waking up from a surgery one time and seeing a kid in the next room lying in a hospital bed. He was actually in a quarantine room.

I could see him through a window. He was about my age and he was bald. At that point in time I had no idea what that meant, that he possibly had cancer. His baldness wasn't significant to me at the time. What I remember most is the John Wayne poster over his bed.

Looking back, I don't know what happened to that kid. I am so blessed to have walked out of surgery, live my life, have my family, and do what I do. I just remember that a cowboy was looking over him and he has been looking over me my whole life. Out of all that ordeal that John Wayne poster is what got me through.

Mark: 11: Now as they approached Jerusalem, near Bethphage and Bethany, at the Mount of Olives, Jesus sent two of his disciples [2] and said to them, "Go to the village ahead of you. As soon as you enter it, you will find a colt tied there that has never been ridden. Untie it and bring it here. ³ If anyone says to you, 'Why are you doing this?' say, 'The Lord needs it and will send it back here soon.'"

In south Alabama, as a cowboy, you get looks. People look at you funny, and essentially, sometimes, spit on you. This resonates with me in terms of Jesus. Jesus was an outsider. He was a hippie. He was not the status "normal" of his time. He stood out. People spit on him. He never spit back. He knew who he was, and he continued his path among the throngs of people cursing and spitting on him. He never cursed back.

I believe this is the great lesson of Jesus. Stay true to yourself. Hold your head high. Know your truth. This is the path of a cowboy.

People think that Jesus had all these super powers. Yes, he was the son of God, but he didn't have super powers. He came to this earth as a man, a human being. He had to suffer through life like the rest of us, like a man. He had to sin for us, and yet, was sinless.

This has been the hardest thing for me to swallow. If someone does me wrong. The hardest thing for me is to not lash out. Jesus wasn't a sissy. But he knew at the end of the day the right path. Yes, he knew he was the son of God, but he was still flesh and blood like you and me.

I believe the biggest take for someone about the fact that Jesus is a cowboy is how steady he was. Just like the Mississippi river, Jesus was steady as you go. He took everything his mortal life threw his way with a grain of salt. We should all aspire to live that way, cowboy cool.

Jesus had no permanent home. Just like your modern-day cowboy. He was essentially a gypsy. He knew his father would provide for him. His faith was so strong. He told his disciples to not take enough bread, water or fish to make it to the next town. It will be provided for you. He said if I am going to feed the birds there to store up for the winter and the lilies of the field in all their splendor, don't you think I am going to take care of you?

Faith without action is not faith at all. You can't just sit in the lazy boy and expect the universe to plop a million dollars in your lap. Jesus acted. He had faith he would be provided for, but he also took the steps to spread love and make sure it happened. This is an example of the best way to live the cowboy way and let Jesus influence your life. Have faith and take action.

Faith is a large part of the cowboy way. When life has you by the hooks. Remember, there is a real cowboy looking over you. Have faith that the best is yet to come.

CHAPTER EIGHT

Cowboy Common Sense (Dollar Stretcher)

I'm not the best in the world, but I'm darn sure not the last. In modern day American life, the goal is to have a nice house, car and boat. People work for forty or fifty years to retire with these things and a big back yard. They take their money and invest in IRAs, mutual funds, stocks and things they cannot see.

They invest their money in this life to see dividends they can leave to their kids or blow in the end. That seems to be the reality of what most people do. There is a sense of keeping up with the Jones' in this.

As a cowboy I don't invest in bonds, mutual funds or IRAs. I do invest in stock: cattle. I can turn cattle into cash on any business day apart from Christmas to the new year. I can take my cows to any stock yard or live stock market any day of the week and sell them.

People invest in their stocks and CDs and they may wait a long time for a return or pay penalties. **That's money the hard way.** A cow is cash. Of course, the cattle market goes up and down. If I pay $1,000 for a momma cow on Monday. She might not be worth but $900 on Tuesday or Wednesday but I can still trade her in for cash if I need to.

I like to invest in something I can see. The land and cattle are tangible. That is how I see **cowboy common sense**. Instead of putting my money into a banker, lawyer or broker's hand for them to invest, I can look at my investment. I can touch it, and I can sell it tomorrow. My son can walk across and scuff his knee on my investment or his future inheritance.

I would rather invest my money in land. The good Lord is not going to make any more of it. I can develop on that land, but nobody is going to make any more of this dirt. Someone may approach me for the next "big thing" investment. I'm not going to put my money in something I don't believe in, something I am not passionate about. I believe in this dirt and what it can provide.

I'm not comfortable putting my hard-earned money that I have blood and sweat in, into the hands of a broker or any middle man to invest for me for the sake of my family. I would rather invest it in something I can walk on, something I can manage myself. **It takes a lot of drops to make a puddle, and I am planning**

on making a pond or maybe a lake. I will build my wealth my way, and you can too.

People tell me you need to invest in this and that. Save it all. Invest in this for 30 years. What happens when you take your last breath? You have your legacy, that's what. What happens to all the investments? We want to leave some to our kids and take care of them, of course. But when you take your last breath, it's kind of about you.

I've been to heaven's door before. If you have trillions of dollars and you're lying there taking your last breath it will not save you. And I promise you, it is not what you think about. You won't be thinking about what kind of car you drove, what school you went to or how big your house was. At that moment in time it's about you.

You don't think about what you left behind. All the movies portray that moment as glorious with flashbacks of your loved ones having a wonderful time. Well, it's bull crap. You are thinking about what's next. I believe the largest investment or decision you will ever make is in, "What's next." What's next after this life?

I revert to the Bible: Anything that you store up, trophies, houses, or cars can be over taken by the earth. Mold, rust, termites, tornadoes or hurricanes can take away your possessions. All of these things are here today and gone tomorrow. We all know that.

Ultimately, a cowboy looks more at his legacy. It is not so much what you do or what you had but what you left behind in terms of your legacy. How did you make people feel while you were here? Even if he works his whole life to hold on to one piece of land a cowboy is investing more in the life hereafter.

Instead of storing up, invest your time in the here and now. When people ask you to invest for the future, there is a future beyond that future. As a cowboy, I believe in the concept of good and evil. Be good. Invest in people.

Growing up, rodeo was all I wanted to do. I ate, drank, slept and breathed rodeo. Every day after school I would come home, eat a snack, change my clothes and start saddling horses and penning my calves.

My dad always worked 10 – 12-hour days, but he always found time to help me practice four to five hours every afternoon. He was, and remains, my biggest hero. I'm hear to tell you that as much as I appreciate that man and all he did for me, when we stepped in the practice pen, you sure kept all the back patting outside.

This was my job and he was my boss and we weren't messing around. My dad always had a saying, "Get your first part," which was nodding your head. In calf roping there are really five simple steps: score, rope, set your slack, flank and tie.

He believed the first was most important, because if that one wasn't done right the rest would not fall into place. This makes perfect sense. It is kind of like building a fence. If your corner braces are not right nothing else matters. That is the foundation, the starting point.

I remember a stretch of time when I wasn't winning anything and couldn't seem to get out of a slump. That's when my dad told me, "You can't keep doing the same thing expecting different results." That one definitely hit home, and was a time in my life that I could have used my **glass belly button**. With my head up my butt I needed it to keep me from walking into traffic.

Common sense is a major factor in what makes cowboys the way they are. It is like our side kick or guardian angel that keeps us from making bad decisions. It tells us **not to pee on an electric fence.** I have heard from second hand experience that the sensation is not what you would expect.

The Bible says, "You reap what you sow." That is about as straight forward and easy to comprehend as it comes. **The odds of you getting kicked by a mule if you slap it on the rear are higher than any casino bet.**

Common sense is like a two-dollar bill, there ain't a whole bunch of them left. I've always heard the saying, "You can't have your cake and eat it too." **This to me makes about as much sense as peeing in the wind.** Listen, if I'm going to take the time to bake or order a cake, I am doing so with every intention of eating it as well.

Common sense ain't that hard y'all. Pull your hat down and be a cowboy. Always have your senses about you. Rally, and if you need to, ask for help. There ain't no shame in it.

CHAPTER NINE

At the end of the Day

If you love what you do everyday then it isn't work. The proof is in the pudding. At the end of most days around here it seems we never really finish our work, we just find a good place to stop.

There is nothing I would rather do after an exhausting day than spend time with Misty and Carter. Without them, the day wouldn't be worth it. After supper and baths; baths are for Misty and Carter by the way. I take showers. It just doesn't make a lick of sense to me to lay in water that you have polluted the minute your foot hits it. Think about it! **Cowboy common sense.**

Anyways, I can't fall asleep until prayers are said, and I kiss my better half and my mini me goodnight and tell them I love them. I try to lie there for a minute and reflect on what happened and what did or didn't get accomplished in the day.

I rarely try to map out the next day because if you farm or ranch you know as well as I do, you won't be able to sleep! Last night I was lying there, thanking the Good Lord for my family, and it came to me, all the blood, sweat and tears that we shed to get to where we want to go don't add up to a hill of beans without family.

The long days and sleepless nights all run into one if we don't have someone to share it with. The Bible says, "You could gain the whole world, but If you forfeit your soul, you've gained nothing." Jesus didn't come to earth to be persecuted, spit on, and crucified for us to spin our wheels. He came for **cowboy love.** He came so we could have life and live it abundantly!

I personally know people that don't know how many cows they have. Not because they have run out of fingers and toes to count them, just because they literally have that many head. Big barns, all the land you can imagine, more deer than you could ever hunt, the nicest vehicles, everything is top notch... But, no one to share it all with except a few "good time friends." It is constant turmoil.

Me, me, me, more, more, more. I'm not saying they are bad people by any means. But if you ask me, which you didn't, I just figured I'd go on and tell you, they are missing the point! I would bet the farm that at the end of the day they would trade every bit of that for a real family. And friends, of course. The kind of people you can sit down with and just talk to and most importantly listen to. The Good Lord gave you two ears and one mouth for a reason!

On the other hand, I know people that don't have much and are just as happy as they can be. They figured out it's not about quantity, it's about quality. My wife and I have been married for four years with a seventeen-month-old baby. Most people can relate how stressful life can be sometimes.

Before we had Carter, we made an oath to each other, **a cowboy contract,** that we would do whatever it took to leave behind a legacy for our kid(s). Whether that be a ranch they could work, a business that they could run, or a better start at life than we had. FYI, we both have amazing parents and had a great start at life. I wouldn't trade my childhood for all the tea in China! But every parent wants to leave their kids better off than they were.

The constant struggle of trying to keep that happy medium between family and success is always a battle. But, it is one worth fighting for. As people, we should be content and thankful for what we have. Now I'm not saying sit around like a knot on a log and hope for the best. Just be content. Take Gus' advice from *Lonesome Dove*, "Don't expect much out of just one thing in life. It's liable to be a disappointment." **Cowboy cool.**

I feel so honored to have the opportunity to write this book. First, my buddies and all my English teachers aren't going to believe it! They must have forgotten about a little thing called autocorrect! It is truly humbling to able to put some thoughts and stories on to paper for people to read and hopefully impact their life.

I have been blessed with positive figures throughout my life and have had opportunities that most folks just read about it. I have gotten to see, first hand, **cowboys be super heroes**. I have seen and been a part of the acts that they portray in movies and songs. It has truly been an honor.

I have had my fair share of mistakes. If you can read this book and it keeps you from making one, then it was well worth it. I have said all that just to say this... bear with me, I'm going to ramble on for just a minute more...

At the end of the day, life is a blessing, I don't give a rats behind what kind of walk of life you come from or what has happened in the past. Put excuses, pity and pride aside and take everything that come across with a grain of salt.

Don't let people or circumstance steal your joy because they or it can't have it unless you give it to them. Don't lose sight of where you came from, no matter where you are going, it doesn't matter if you have a million dollars or just two wooden nickels. Stay humble.. Look straight ahead at the important things in life like faith, family, and friends.

You are going to reap what you sow. If you work hard and are patient good things will come. I guarantee you that. Always remember, people are watching even when you think they aren't. You are a role model to someone, whether you realize it or not. It is up to you to make a positive impact on them. Finally, life is going to get you down, it's inevitable. Don't let it keep you there. It is a choice! When you think that you can't go anymore just remember there is a father in heaven that loves you. What he brings you to, he'll bring you through. When it is all said and done, at the end of the day, dust yourself off, pick your head up, pull your hat down and be a cowboy!

When in doubt go the cowboy route.

Cody Harris, his wife Misty Harris, and his son Carter Harris.

Made in the USA
Coppell, TX
25 September 2020